written for all the
children who love
exploring the
outdoors

ONCE UPON A TIME IN A MEADOW SO GREEN, VISITED SPARK, THE LITTLEST STAR EVER SEEN.

IN THE DEWY GRASS WERE FLOWERS SO BRIGHT, SPARK DECIDED TO HUNT BUGS BY NIGHT.

[redacted] [redacted]

A CRICKET CHIRPED WITH A MELODY SO CLEAR, SPARK HID BEHIND A DAISY, QUITE NEAR.

PEEKING OUT AT THE CRICKET'S SONG, SPARK WATCHED QUIETLY ALL NIGHT LONG.

NEXT CAME A LADYBIRD, RED WITH BLACK SPOTS,
SPARK TWINKLED SOFTLY, CONNECTING DOTS.

ON A DAISY IN THE MOON'S SOFT GLOW,
SPARK STARED AT THE LADYBIRD, MOVING SLOW.

SOME FIREFLIES BLINKED WITH A LIGHT SO BRIGHT, SPARK TWINKLED BACK, DELIGHTING IN THE SIGHT.

TOGETHER THEY DANCED IN THE NIGHTTIME AIR, TWO LITTLE LIGHTS, A GLOWING PAIR.

SOME ANTS MARCHED ON WITH A PURPOSE, STRONG AND NEAT, SPARK STARED IN AWE, FEELING THEIR BEAT.

WATCHING THE ANTS WORK WITH SUCH GRACE, SPARK LEARNED THE VALUE OF A STEADY PACE.

A SPIDER WEAVED A WEB, DELICATE AND GRAND, SPARK MARVELLED AT THE ART, CLOSE AT HAND.

GLISTENING THREADS IN THE MOONLIGHT GLEAM, SPARK ADMIRED THE SPIDER'S WOVEN DREAM.

A BUTTERFLY FLUTTERED WITH WINGS SO BRIGHT, SPARK FOLLOWED CLOSELY, LOVING THE SIGHT.

IN A MEADOW FULL, OF FLOWERS SWEET, SPARK AND THE BUTTERFLY TOOK A SEAT.

A BEETLE SCUTTLED WITH ARMOUR SO TOUGH, SPARK ADMIRED ITS COURAGE, BOLD AND ROUGH.

TOGETHER THEY EXPLORED THE GRASSY FLOOR, SPARK FOUND NEW FRIENDS AND WISHED FOR MORE.

AS THE BUG HUNT CONTINUED THROUGHOUT THE NIGHT, SPARK SHONE UNTIL DAWN, A COMFORTING LIGHT.

WITH EACH INSECT NOW, A FRIEND SO DEAR, SPARK SHONE BRIGHTLY, SPREADING SOME CHEER.

NOW, DEAR READER,
THE HUNT IS COMPLETE,
I HOPE YOU ENJOYED
THE BIG BUG RETREAT.

NOW LOOK BACK AT
THE PICTURES, AND
SPOT SPARK'S GLEAM, A
SHINING FRIEND IN
EVERY SCENE.

SOUVENIR

WHICH BUG WAS YOUR FAVOURITE FROM OUR BUG HUNT?

I LIKED THE FIREFLIES
AND THE WAY THEY
LIT UP THE SKY
WITH THEIR
DANCING

CRICKET
LADYBIRD
FIREFLY
ANT
SPIDER
BUTTERFLY
BEETLE

Printed in Great Britain
by Amazon

48248864R00016